Ultimate Sailing

Ultimate Sailing

Sharon Green

with Douglas Hunter

FIREFLY BOOKS

A Firefly Book

Published in the United States in 1998 by
Firefly Books (U.S.) Inc.
P.O. Box 1338, Ellicott Station
Buffalo, New York, USA
14205

Cataloging in Publication Data

Green, Sharon, 1960–
Ultimate sailing

ISBN 1-55209-249-6

1. Sailing – Pictorial works. 2. Yachting – Pictorial works.
I. Hunter, Douglas, 1959– II. Title.

GV811.G733 1998a   797.1'24'0222   C98-930522-8

Published by arrangement with
Stoddart Publishing Co. Limited

Ultimate Sailing™ is a trademarked title (registration
pending) by Sharon Green, Windward Productions Inc.,
P.O. Box 1063, Southport, Connecticut, 06490
www.ultimatesailing.com
For marine trade and corporate sales
Tel. (203) 254-3033 Fax. (203) 254-2076

Text and jacket design: Andrew Smith Graphics Inc.

Printed and bound in Hong Kong, China by
Book Art Inc., Toronto

To my parents, Donald and Sandy Green, who gave me inspiration, opportunity, and ambition. In memory of my grandfather Green, whose spirit of adventure rides the seas with me. To Cary Peirce, my friend and business associate, without whose expertise and dedication Windward Productions wouldn't run. And to my family and friends for their encouragement, love, and support.

SHARON GREEN

Contents

Acknowledgments 9

Introduction 10

Turning Points 15

All Hands 49

Redlining 79

Water Colors 105

Tangles of Angles 125

Flying Colors 147

Derigging 166

Plate Notes 167

Acknowledgments

Special thanks to Stoddart Publishing and the unflappable and always enthusiastic Mike Wallace, who for the last sixteen years has overseen the production of the *Ultimate Sailing* calendar and now, finally, the book. I am also grateful to Doug Hunter for interpreting my images and expressing in words the essence of Ultimate Sailing. Thanks as well to the numbers of boat drivers and pilots whose long hours and expert skills help make it all happen.

Introduction

THERE IS SAILING, AND THEN THERE IS ULTIMATE SAILING. THERE is the knockabout dinghy at the cottage dock, and then there is the Maxi boat with a crew of two dozen, an operating budget larger than that of most small businesses, and an itinerary that

spans the globe. Ultimate Sailing is everywhere, but not just *anywhere*. You will find it in selected locales, like Newport, Rhode Island; Cowes, England; San Francisco, California; Oahu, Hawaii; Auckland, New Zealand; and Fremantle, Australia. It is a traveling circus, a spectacle playing simultaneously under several big tops. And, strangely for such a big event, the spectator is welcomed, but not necessarily sought after. I found my own way to the show, and with these photographs I invite you along.

As enormously popular as it is in certain corners of the globe, and among diehard fanatics everywhere, sailing has never been a major league spectator sport. It is not the National Football League or World Cup soccer, and it never will be. But the beauty of sailing is that the sport has reached such impressive heights of excellence and sophistication on the strength of its self-regard. Sailors have *always* been sailing's greatest fans. They have made the sport what it is through their own devotion and their willingness, in many cases, to make it the focal point of their lives. Sponsorship and cash competitions have come to sailing, but they have not in and of themselves created what we call Ultimate Sailing. That credit belongs to the boat owners, race organizers, and sailors whose ambitions have created one of the greatest sporting shows on earth. And slowly but surely, the general public has become fascinated with the show, lured at first, perhaps, by glimpses of the America's Cup, the Whitbread Round the World Race, or a major regatta on their own waterfront. In this age dominated by corporate dollars, it is nothing less than a marvel that an endeavor as magnificent as this, as complex as anything motor sports can offer, has come to thrive without having television and marketing rights as prerequisites to its existence.

It is a romantic sport. Sailing pits sailors not only against each other, individually and in teams, but also against the elements. And in reality it is not carried out "against" the elements — in the way that baseball is sometimes played in the rain — but *because* of them. Sailing is a technological response to wind and waves that requires both ingenuity and courage. For those who are captivated by it, the challenge is its own reward. Whether anyone else is watching is irrelevant. Ultimate Sailing does not exist to put on a show.

But what a show. What a riot of color — and what a noise! Ultimate Sailing does not have a soundtrack of gentle breezes and burbling waters. It crackles with the snapping and lashing of sails, chatters and clatters with whirling winches, booms with powerful hulls punching through seas. It is a sport that can leave you hoarse, from simply making yourself heard to shipmates and opponents.

The pictures that follow are outwardly silent, but I would like them to convey this sonic energy, as much as their stillness is meant to communicate motion, transition, anticipation, and apprehension. If you sail, I hope these pictures take you to familiar places. If you have never sailed, perhaps they will impart to you a sense of what it must be like.

Ultimate Sailing is a highly polished world of serious fun. This is not a realm of picturesque teak decks and brass fittings. Ultimate Sailing looks the way the United States Air Force would if it were given to civilians to run for the fun of it. It is a world of sophisticated and dazzling materials: of Kevlar and Mylar; fiberglass and carbon fiber; titanium, aluminum, stainless steel, and cobalt. It is a world of utilitarian beauty, adorned with colors and graphics intended not to sell some product, but to sell its own sense of spectacle.

Ultimate Sailing is a grand fraternity. Its members are friends and rivals, sharing a camaraderie that comes from traversing the globe and pursuing excellence in different events in different yachts. Before skippers Dennis Conner and John Bertrand met in the historic America's Cup match of 1983, they had represented their countries at the 1976 Olympics and sailed together in an SORC campaign. They are not unusual. Careers crisscross, converge, and diverge. The great talents in the world of Ultimate Sailing park their ditty bags in everything that floats, from Olympic Finns to America's Cup 75-footers to round-the-world racers. The people, as much as the events and the yachts, make up the circus.

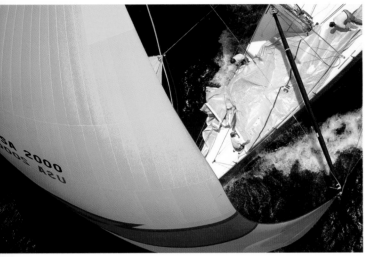

Ultimate Sailing is a show with no firm itinerary. Different disciplines, different groups of boats, have their own regatta schedules, but the talents aboard them move from one schedule to another, binding the show together into a coherent whole. They're aboard a 45-foot IMS boat for the French team at the Admiral's Cup in the Solent; at a Maxi regatta off Newport; serving as tactician on an ultralight sled in San Francisco; polishing an Olympic Soling program; and signing on with an America's Cup challenge syndicate.

What makes these Ultimate Sailors roam the globe? Certainly for most it isn't to swell their bank accounts. While prize money is available at some elite events, and the circuit has its share of paid hands and industry professionals, most sailors are there for the love of a sport that has no equal. The breadth and depth of yacht racing is astonishing. If something is powered by the wind, someone is going to want to race it. For most sailors, though, the Big Show, the Ultimate Sailing Circus, is one they can but dream of joining. It requires extraordinary commitment from participants who must otherwise try to live normal lives. They must be among the very best in a demanding and often dangerous game. They must set personal goals that are not only attainable, but also desirable. Perching on the rail of a 50-footer, smashing through cold seas, is not everyone's idea of a good time. Ultimate Sailing is a challenge accepted and extended. It's not enough to want to do it — you must also want to do it better than anyone else.

It's a circus that has to be seen to be believed. I've been watching it for almost twenty years. Here's a bit of what I've seen.

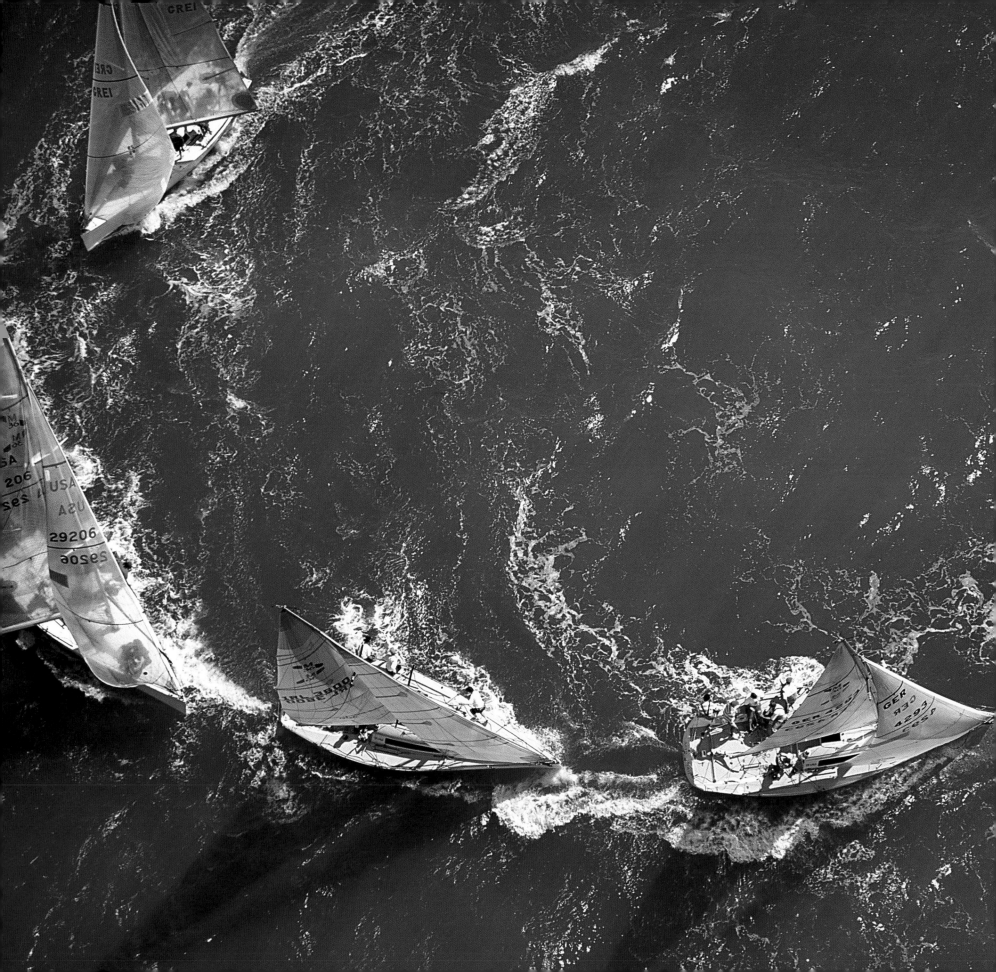

Turning Points

YACHT RACING MEASURES ITS COURSES IN NAUTICAL MILES AND ITS opportunities in boatlengths. Mark roundings are the sport's most explosive transition points, where boat handling and crew skills are tested thoroughly in a few seconds of decisive choreography. A spinnaker hoisted too slowly, a sail overtrimmed, a skipper who steers a few feet off the perfect trajectory — miscues that might be minor aspects of the rest of the race are potential disasters as a fleet converges on a buoy. A crew that has struggled to eke out every extra boatlength on its opponents along a lengthy leg of the course can see it all erased by a momentary error. The mark rounding is an arena of attack and defense; aggression is rewarded, even demanded, as windows of opportunity open and all too quickly close. The finest hull design, the fastest sails, can make no difference if a turning point becomes more than a mark — if it becomes an opportunity squandered, an advantage surrendered.

MUCH OF THE ACTION IN YACHT RACING IS UNPREDICTABLE. MARK roundings are an exception, and they give me the opportunity to position myself in a set location, where I know a transition will occur. There are many angles and a quiver of equipment to choose from. Depending on the fleet, the direction of approach, and the direction of the turn, I will set up to have the action either coming towards me or going away. This control is a rare luxury — I can see how the boats are approaching and estimate their turn — but there is always an element of surprise. The photo boat driver has quite a job dealing with current, wind, and other spectator craft while holding the boat in position.

Gybe ho: a trio of Maxis parades around a mark (above). Bladerunner "teabags" the spinnaker during a takedown (right).

The bowman on a hurtling 50-footer seeks refuge behind the jib, bearing the brunt of the preparations for a heavy-air spinnaker hoist.

It's all downhill from here: Atalanti churns around the windwark mark (left). Yachts stack up like 737s over La Guardia as they negotiate the turn (right).

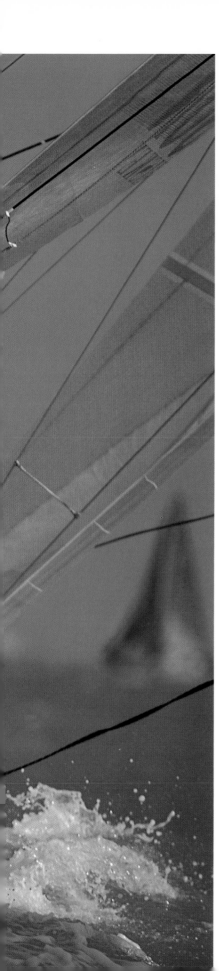

Calamity confronts the crew as the spinnaker goes AWOL during a leeward mark rounding (left). A descending spinnaker hovers over the sea in a frantic takedown (above).

Apprehension dictates the body language of the crew as Faster K-Yote *careens into a spinnaker set (left). The Maxi yachts* Sorcery, Il Moro, Ondine, *and* Matador *bear down on the gybe mark (below).*

The turning mark looms like a wayward planet as the Mumm 36 Corum gives hot pursuit at the leeward mark (left). The eagle is landing: the spinnaker begins its descent nearing the leeward mark (right).

> *Sailing teams are not really different from any other team in sport. Football has its quarterbacks, linemen, and receivers; we have helmsmen, grinders, and bowmen. All are trained to do their jobs not as individuals but as part of a team. That is the greatest and perhaps most challenging aspect of big boat racing: getting the team performance right. The more a team practises, the better it will be. Not every play or spinnaker set will be perfect, but there is a magic that comes when it does. There is little that can compare. The trick is to make every maneuver have that same magic.*
>
> *Oh, by the way: when it goes wrong, it really goes WRONG!*

ROD DAVIS, TWO-TIME OLYMPIC MEDALIST,
AMERICA'S CUP HELMSMAN, WORLD CLASS SAILOR

Cleanup detail: the crew of Rubin *prepares for battle to windward, looking for opportunities while closing the door on pursuers.*

A Roy Lichtenstein mermaid graces the hull of Young America, 1995 America's Cup defense contender (left). A crewman in the "sewer" considers how much more chute will be joining him in a confused takedown (right).

America's Cup 12-Metres experience a full dose of Indian Ocean breeze from the Fremantle Doctor as New Zealand leads the fleet into the leeward mark at the 1986 12-Metre Worlds in Western Australia.

The downwind sled ride becomes a jackhammer turn to windward in Hawaiian wind and waves.

A pair of competitors approaching the
windward mark slices through the wake
of an opponent that is already around
and setting the spinnaker (left). The
crew of Heaven Can Wait has the chute
up and running as a competitor makes
its windward mark approach (right).

A falcon's-eye view of a "floater drop"
spinnaker takedown (above). IOR 50s
stack up in a succession of quarter-wakes
off Sardinia (right).

All Hands

SAILING IS A HIGH-WIRE ACT, A CRAFT OF TIMING, DARING, FINESSE, and defiance. Level heads are required in a world that has little time for the horizontal. Great sailors master intricate routines that at any moment may have to be abandoned for improvisation. Great crews know each member's role intimately; they can stand backwards, close their eyes, and do their jobs together seamlessly. They marry a mastery of theory and technology with physical dexterity. They immerse themselves in probability, weighing the merits of tactical choices, with one eye out for potential disaster. They take risks without being foolhardy. They rely on each other. Their bonds cross decks, fleets, and oceans. As the banquet toast goes, *To sailors everywhere!*

No pain, no gain: Brad Dellenbaugh, Stever Calder, and Dave Curtis hang out in heavy seas to keep their Soling driving to windward (above), while Olympic silver medalists Rod Davis and Don Cowie endure the spray kicked up by their Star off Kiel, Germany (right).

CAPTURING A DEFINITIVE MOMENT IN THE DUTIES OF A SINGLE CREWMEMBER, or the harmony of an entire crew, ranks among the most difficult photographic challenges. Often it is simply luck that has allowed me to freeze a slice of time that can illuminate the challenges sailors face, the risks they take, the strains they bear. The shot at the opening of this chapter is from aboard the J-Class yacht *Endeavour*. I was up on the bow, shooting back towards the crew, when out of the corner of my eye I caught the bowman gathering the momentum to push himself to reach the end of the spinnaker pole to lead a new sheet. My exposure wasn't set for the conditions. I just guessed, opened up the F-stop two stops, and fired. The result was this one frame, perfectly exposed.

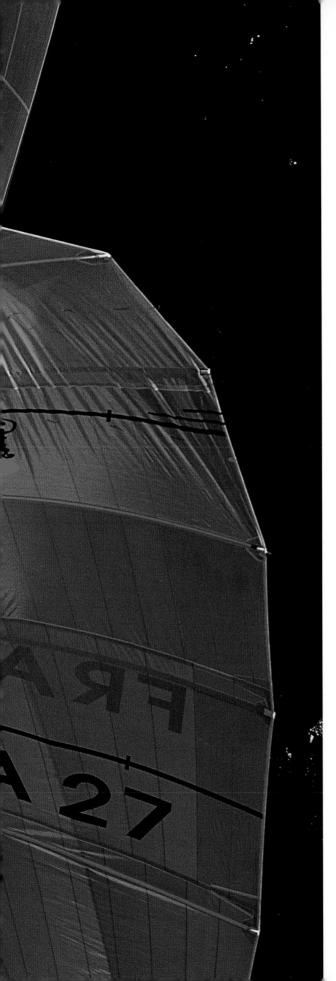

> *Three minutes of furious activity and a smart float drop later, we are*
> *pounding away upwind again. The foredeck is cleaned up, the chute is*
> *packed, and I am back on the rail, contemplating the next move. We've got*
> *a five-boatlength lead; the next leg is a reach. I check the wind, ten*
> *degrees left. The first reach will be tight, might even be the 2.2 oz. Possibly*
> *too close for the staysail, we'll have it ready anyway. We're out on the left*
> *side of the course, probably two more tacks to a tack set. I've got a couple*
> *of minutes to catch my breath so that — the jib breaks! I'm rushing for-*
> *ward . . . Fortunately, we have anticipated this, too . . .*

SCOTT VOGEL, WORLD-CLASS BOWMAN, THREE-TIME AMERICA'S CUP CREW

It's lonely at the top: repair duties send a sailor to the
very heights of the America's Cup experience (left).
The spinnaker is loaded for launching aboard 1995
America's Cup winner Team New Zealand (above).

Etchells sailors ride the rocking horse on the windward leg (above). The spinnaker is on the way down, with only seconds in which to gather it aboard before it touches the water and becomes a sea anchor (right).

A Maxi crewmember draws the dangerous assignment of freeing a jammed halyard (left). The world seems a blur in an Olympic-class Tornado operating at full throttle (right).

The spinnaker is set and drawing as the bowman clears away the last few inches of the great genoa aboard an America's Cup challenger (left). A Maxi yacht punches a very large hole in the Gulf Stream (right).

A high-wire act: Australian 18-Foot Skiff sailors can barely be considered aboard their boat as they trapeze from its hiking rack, using their weight and tremendous leverage to keep the craft upright and flying.

*Crowd control: all hands ride the rail
and urge the 66-foot Exile through
punishing waves. Only a few people
are on the job; the rest are enjoying an
assignment as human ballast.*

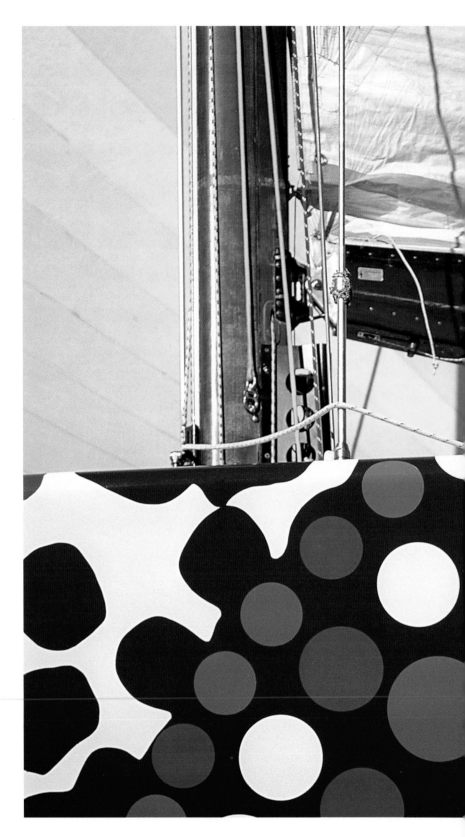

A descending spinnaker keeps a small crowd of sailors busy after a new one has been set (above). A testing session gives two Australian America's Cup sailors a rare chance to relax (right).

The clubhouse turn: a fleet of Solings goes for broke as it rides a fresh breeze to the finish line (left). Dennis Conner brings the America's Cup back from Down Under at the helm of Stars & Stripes *in the 1987 match (above).*

The chase is on as opponents duel for position downwind (left). Sail trimming is a proverbial grind as fine-tuning demands total concentration, regardless of what's in your face (above).

The bowman aboard the 54-foot Jubilation *tends to the Gordian knot of rope and wire at the business end of the spinnaker pole during a sail change.*

Eyes and ears: an International America's Cup Class bowman calls the start for an afterguard some seventy feet behind him (above). The entire crew of this 50-footer is on the rail, but it looks like they could still use a dozen friends to help their yacht find its feet (right).

Redlining

THERE ARE NO BRAKES, NO PARACHUTES, NO BUTTONS TO STOP THE ride so you can get off. When a boat's performance is maxed out, nothing is holding it back. The crew is operating at the razor's edge of control; the boat is in a groove that is as narrow as it is grease-slick. You've pushed the corners of the performance envelope, licked the stamp, and dispensed with the return address.

Boats on the outside edge of control are "meta-stable" — the slightest perturbation in the precarious equilibrium of forces driving them forward sends them into the realm of chaos theory. An extra breath of wind, an almost imperceptible change in the waves, a small error on board: any one of these can trigger a chain reaction culminating in a full-fledged crash-and-burn scenario.

It's remarkable how quiet the world is when it's all over.

THE PHOTOGRAPHER CAPTURING A BOAT IN MAXED-OUT CONDITIONS — FRAMING that one elusive moment by being in the right place at the right time — often faces more danger and difficulty than the sailors being photographed. In "big" conditions (strong wind, big waves), I'd rather be on a sailboat than on a chase boat. But as I have always said, as we pound through the seas in the chase boat: the wetter and more miserable I am, the better the photos. Once, I was caught in the windward quarter-wake from a fleet of boats streaking along a reach. The chase boat I was in was too small for the conditions, and we capsized.

Another time I was in Newport, Rhode Island, determined to get out to a downwind finish of a Maxi boat regatta, despite dangerous conditions. We bashed through huge seas, walls of water that occasionally broke over the boat and threatened to swamp it. We did make it out and I was able to catch the boats as they screamed downwind to the finish. It was so rough and wet that I couldn't possibly use a big lens. The yachts *Il Moro* and *Longobarda* were neck and neck; *Il Moro* started to luff up *Longobarda*. I instinctively knew this was trouble (for them) and opportunity (for me).

I yanked my camera with a short zoom out of the waterproof box, just as I heard a deafening breaking sound, and was able to catch the dramatic rig-breaking sequence on pages 92–93. Concentrating on focus, exposure, and keeping spray off the lens, I had no idea what I had caught until I viewed the slides. Only then did I see the sailor in flight off the boat's stern.

We pounded so hard that day that every time we came off a wave, the boat shuddered and uttered a horrible noise. I kept wondering if we had cracked the hull. Sure enough, it sank at the dock that night.

There are a few rare, exhilarating days when the conditions are prime — it's clear, windy (over eighteen knots), and the seas are rough. On these exceptional days, especially if it's an important event like the America's Cup, the adrenaline flows. Gearing up, preparing to leave the dock or heliport, I pray for all the mechanical things (the boat or helicopter, all the equipment) to behave. There is a lot of pressure on these spectacular days because they rarely happen. One day like this can produce many significant images.

Of course, there are nice photos that can be taken on days when the wind is light, but the action really happens when the wind velocity is up and the boats spring to life and take on a completely different character, complete with power, spray, and speed.

Some twenty-seven tons of 12-Metre thunder across an angry Indian Ocean (above). Maxi yachts push each other into the far corner of the performance envelope (right).

" *Ironically, when you are sailing at full speed, you actually want to be frozen in time so the sensation never ends. When you are on top of a wave, sailboats are remarkably stable. Without question, these moments are the highlights of the sport.* "

GARY JOBSON, AUTHOR, ESPN COMMENTATOR, WINNING AMERICA'S CUP TACTICIAN

Surf's up: Georgia has found perfect balance in Hawaiian seas (left). Etchells sailors take their 30-foot keelboat for a ride in Atlantic swells (above).

A fleet of Melges 24s sets asymmetrical spinnakers before a surplus of horsepower on San Francisco Bay (left). Meanwhile, on another part of the bay, an International 14 trips over itself during a maneuver, leaving helmsman Ed Baird gasping for air (above).

Incoming: a crewmember is catapulted off the stern as the rig comes down on the Maxi Longobarda, *sending about eighteen people diving for cover.*

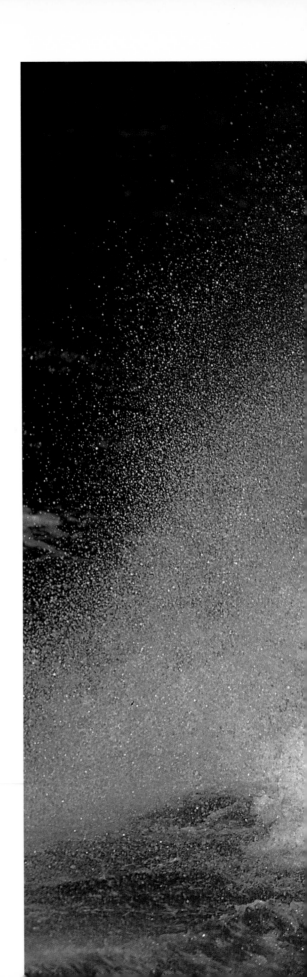

Big waves, low freeboard: a Melges 30 "submarines" off Miami (above). Icy spray explodes from bow to stern as a 36-footer tests Atlantic rollers (right).

*A posse of Melges 24s gallops across
San Francisco Bay (left). Rivals
take to the air in a duel to the
windward mark off Hawaii (above).*

The Maxi Boomerang whips San Francisco Bay into meringue on a close reach (left). A "hard water" aficionado carves a trajectory across Massachusetts ice (above).

*Spinnaker, headsail, and mainsail shift a Maxi
into overdrive (above). America's Cup 12-Metres
catch rides on each other's stern waves (right).*

Winsome Gold *scores a "10" for artistic impression and a "1.2" for technical merit as she executes a spectacular crash-and-burn wipeout.*

Water Colors

SOME OF THE GREATEST PAINTERS WERE DRAWN TO THE SEA. THE Impressionists, whose devotion was to light rather than form, color rather than line, could look upon it and find profound inspiration. The attraction in the seascape was not the precise contour of a hull, an exact representation of rigging, a perfect accounting of wave crests and troughs; instead, the painters were drawn to its broad strokes of color, its delicate points of light, its subtle transition of tones.

Sometimes a spinnaker is just a spinnaker. And sometimes it is a water lily in Monet's eye.

WHEN I BEGAN PHOTOGRAPHING YACHT RACING AS A TEENAGER, I WAS NOT conscious of composition. On the water, I was struggling with equipment, the elements, exposure, focus, the action, directing the boat driver, and loading film in wild conditions. I would shoot all day, not even remembering what had passed across the viewfinder to make me press the shutter. When the film was processed, I was often startled by the composition I had achieved in a particular image. I hadn't been aware of whether I was holding the camera vertically or horizontally. It was just instinct. My early work truly was artistic, because I didn't know any better.

The camera and lens create a narrow point of view. Whether I'm hanging out of a helicopter or shooting from a chase boat, what I see and shoot can be happening in hundredths of a second. The rectangular window presents a frame through which I allow the action to pass. When I see an interesting composition, I fire. At the end of the day I often feel like I witness the event with tunnel vision.

The Maxis Kialoa, Boomerang, *and* Ragamuffin *march across a sparkling ocean, their crews seeming to walk on waves (left). A lifting fog bank reveals a headsail switch underway on San Francisco Bay as a yacht's crew responds to the changing weather (above).*

J-Boats are a paradigm of absolute yacht-ness. They are long, and low, and deep, with a sweeping sheer and a towering rig. They are flush deck, so the helmsman has an unimpeded view across a hundred feet of teak. They are massive, with seventy tons of lead in the keel and tremendous sail area — 17,000 square feet with the spinnaker up.

More than anything else, J-Boats are beautiful. Of course I am besotted, but I think the case can be made that J-Boats are the most glorious objects ever created by man. "

ELIZABETH MEYER, PRESIDENT,
J-CLASS MANAGEMENT AND INTERNATIONAL
YACHT RESTORATION SCHOOL

America's Cup 12-Metres carve the ocean into deeply veined marble off Fremantle, Australia (left). An America's Cup era of varnished wood and acres of canvas is conjured by the revitalized J-Class Shamrock *(right).*

*America's Cup contender
one*Australia *dares a storm front
during training (left).
A groundswell masks a spinnaker
drop at a leeward rounding (right).*

I love a parade: Mumm 36s in an international fleet find elbow room on a run through the Strait of Florida (above and right).

Espana's logo brightens the prospects of her crew as the International America's Cup Class yacht prepares for a day of competition (left). A Mumm 36 bids the sun goodnight in a race into darkness off Hawaii.

America's Cup contender oneAustralia
*merges with wind and wave (left). Liquid
jade yields to the upwind ambitions of a
trio of SORC competitors (above).*

*Heavy traffic: Maxi yachts tow their wave
trains through a fleet of smaller Kenwood
Cup competitors (above). The swells of
Rhode Island Sound undulate through an
international fleet of Etchells (right).*

Shockwave rides the waves, turning the ocean's energy to its advantage (left), while a thoroughbred fleet of Stars meets the aggressive chop of Biscayne Bay with equal determination (above).

Tangles of Angles

WHEN SAILORS ENCOUNTERED THE WIRES AND STRUTS OF INNOVATIVE one-piece masts at the turn of the century, they thought "Marconi" — as in the transmission towers of Guglielmo Marconi, the Italian radio pioneer — and the name stuck. These Marconi contraptions gave a fresh geometry to the sport, as tall, triangular sails began parading around triangular courses. The physics of sailing, the need to tack back and forth to make progress to windward, made these wire-lashed shapes converge and diverge, overlap and intertwine, as tacticians worked shifting winds to find the shortest distance along an indirect path. The management of tremendous loads fell to ever more exotic materials — Kevlar in line, solid cobalt in rigging — transforming support structures into finely drawn lines of tension that crystallized the picture plane. Sailing became a festival of geometry, lines and shapes in motion, and everyone angling for an advantage.

EARLY ON, I KNEW MY STYLE WAS NOT ABOUT BOAT PORTRAITS. I WOULD see intricate shapes and patterns and respond to something entirely different from a boat sailing along. I was drawn to symmetry, graceful angles, textures, a riot of color — the visual elements the sport brought to the lens. There's no doubt that a good action shot is often the most impressive image, but with all the traveling I do, with all the endless hours on the water at so many events, I probably only have one opportunity in a year to produce a dramatic image from extreme conditions. The rest of the time, I'm out there shooting, and the challenge is to create something out of what I'm given. It's not a case of making the best of a bad situation. Rather, it's a case of taking the raw material given to you and creating something that is memorable in its own right.

Room and opportunity:
Maxi yachts gybe through
the fleet with feet to spare.

A Maxi fleet pursues an empty horizon on the Strait of Florida (above). Alcatraz prison appears to leave no means of escape as opponents cross tacks (right).

The elegant architecture of sail power overshadows the muscle and machinery that contrive to control it (left). The deceptively simple engineering of iceboats poised for a start belies the thruway speeds they can generate at a moment's notice (right).

" *The tactics and strategy of sailboat racing are like playing a game of chess in three dimensions. First, there's the challenge of interpreting and predicting wind and currents — you could win virtually every race if you could pick the right path to follow. But good old Mother Nature doesn't like being too predictable, as any weatherman knows. Then there's the competition — a cunning bunch — who are trying to use the exhaust from their sails (and sometimes the hulls of their boats) to hold you back. Finally, there's the race course: simply finding the next turning mark in low visibility can drive the best navigator crazy. All in all, it's a great and challenging game that rewards the cleverest (and sometimes luckiest) sailor with victory.* "

PETER ISLER, AMERICA'S CUP WINNER,
AUTHOR, TELEVISION COMMENTATOR

An upwind drag race produces mirrors of concentration in helmsmen, their attention fixed on seas and sails.

An irresistible force contemplates an immovable object: a crew appears to look for guidance from solid rock on when to tack to avoid it (left). A 49-footer puts the shore behind it in a hitch out to sea (right).

A fleet of 50-footers leans as one into the task of securing the best position for the imminent start, their crews shouting instructions among themselves and warnings to each other.

A forest of rigging grows from a windward mark convergence (above). Yachts merge into a single wind-driven marvel, united in determination to outperform each other (right).

*The melée of prestart maneuvers
distills into a synchronous
determination to get on with winning
as the starting gun sounds (left). Sails
crowd the skies on a close-fought
spinnaker reach (above).*

*Iceboats draw a horizon of sharks'
teeth across a bright, cold day (left). A
freighter mimics the permanence of a
headland as sailors give ample room
to both (above).*

Flying Colors

THERE WAS A TIME WHEN SAILING ADHERED TO A PALETTE RUNNING from white to cream, with stops along the way at ivory and linen. No longer: now the sport is a floating Mardi Gras, alive to the possibilities of extravagant beauty. Off the wind, yachts sport spinnakers that dazzle, energized by the wind and a spectrum of color. These riotous sails — free-flying, pulsing, crackling with energy rather than billowing — convincingly argue that power, grace, and speed deserve to be color-coded. Red is hot. Blue is cool. And green is envy.

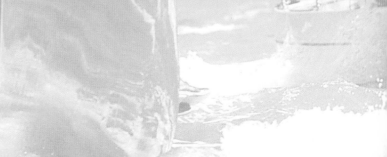

Asymmetrical spinnakers infuse a fleet with a surfeit of energy (above). Blue on blue: a new spinnaker is led into position for hoisting (right).

COLOR AND INTERESTING COMPOSITION ARE THE KEY ELEMENTS IN SOME of my favorite shots, and aerial photography days often provide me with the best opportunities to produce the most memorable and abstract images. It is critical to time an aerial day with the conditions. It must be sunny and breezy.

Photographing sailing from a helicopter is an art in itself. I love to fly! Even with its expense and inherent dangers (and I've had a few close calls), I prefer to shoot from the air. Just as working from a photo boat requires a skilled driver, shooting from a helicopter demands a good pilot. I also try to be conscious of the noise and downdraft we create, and it helps if the pilot knows a bit about sailing. The time in the air is intense, and goes by remarkably fast: an hour contracts into what seems like a few minutes.

My first aerial shoot was of the seventh and deciding race of the 1983 America's Cup between *Australia II* and *Liberty*. I was sharing a Bell Jet Ranger with a colleague, and I'll never forget the feeling of detachment. In the air, you are entirely removed from the action. The sound of the rotor blades and engine vibration drown out the camera shutters and any exterior noise. *Australia II* crossed the finish line and smoke puffed from the race committee boat's finish gun, bringing an end to America's 132-year domination of the trophy. The spectator fleet went wild, and I could see, but not feel, the pandemonium. I commented over the intercom to my colleague that we had just witnessed a huge event in sporting history, and yet we were so far removed from it. I remember shaking, probably from the cold air swirling through the open doors, but also from nerves.

The bloopers break out on San Francisco Bay as sailors strive to distill every available ounce of thrust from a generous breeze.

The crew is positioned as perfectly as the
sails and hull as they streak downwind
(left). The angry comb of an Atlantic
roller gives physical dimension to the
wind energy pressing the sails of a One
Design 48 fleet (above).

A strong, steady wind molds spinnakers into shapes that seem as solid as the hulls beneath them (left). The chute is still on the way up but already drawing persuasively as the crew hurries to stay one step ahead of its efforts (above).

Taut sails haul 12-Metres across a boisterous ocean (left). The expansive spinnaker of an International America's Cup Class yacht displays the sailmaker's ingenuity in creating perfect structures out of nothing more than meticulously shaped seams (right).

*A 50-footer gathers steam for the
assault on the next wave (above). The
spinnaker of the 80-foot* Boomerang
*looms like a dirigible above its quarry,
the 78-foot* Falcon 2000 *(right).*

" *The spinnaker delivers a visceral sense of sailing's power. The least restrained of all sails, it can literally crackle with energy in a breeze. The power of the wind is never more plainly harnessed. When set and sheeted properly, it is a beautiful, almost living thing. When it gets a mind of its own, though, it can be like a wild animal on the end of a lasso without enough cowboys to tame it.* "

TOM WHIDDEN, WORLD CLASS SAILOR,
SAILMAKER, AND AMERICA'S CUP WINNER

Big, bigger, biggest: One Design 48s measure themselves against the Golden Gate Bridge as they regiment their progress across the picture plane (above). Maxi crewmembers take time for foredeck housekeeping, clearing away the genoa that gave way to the spinnaker that dwarfs them (right).

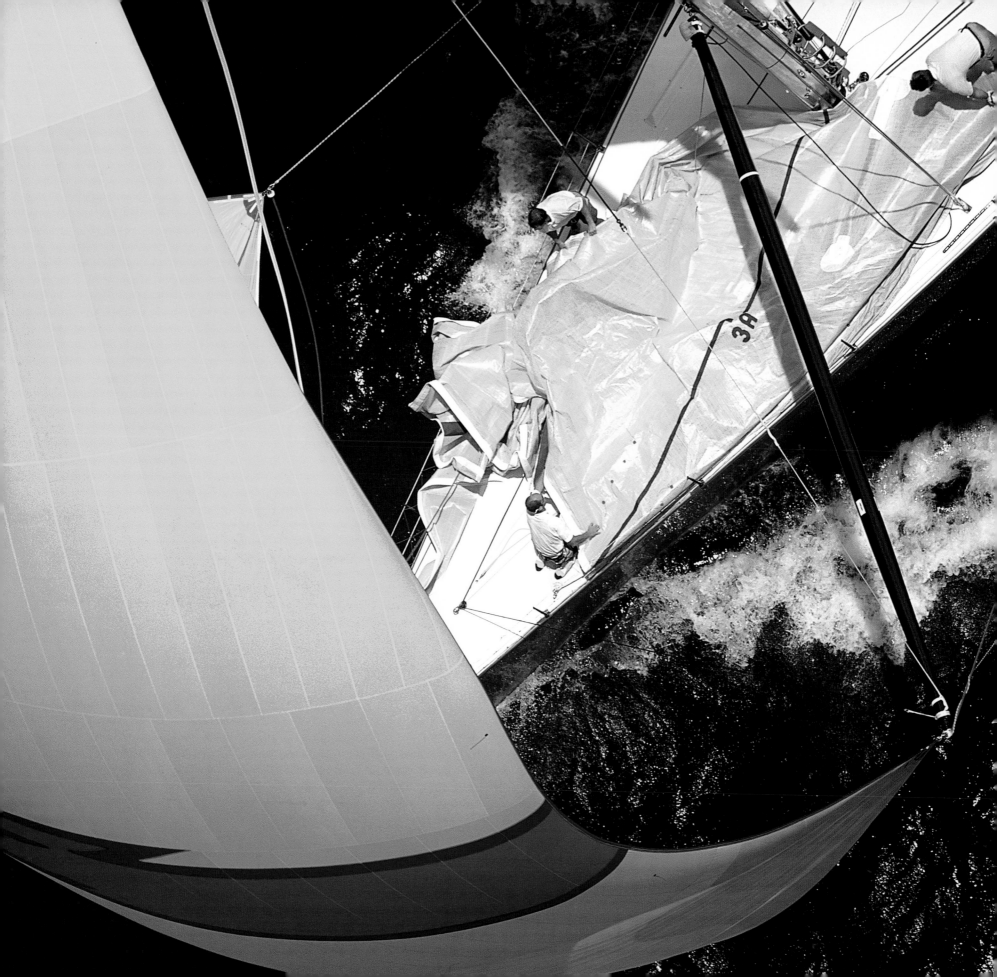

Competitors are in perfect agreement on direction
and trim — and, no doubt, their prospects for
success — in a reach across San Francisco Bay (left).
The blunt contours of the spinnaker drive the knife
edge of the bow of America's Cup winner America[3].

"Big boats" on San Francisco Bay move aside thousands of gallons of water as their spinnakers rein in thousands of cubic feet of air (above). A 47-footer's destroyer bow erupts from a swell off Miami, showing no restraint of purpose of passage (right).

Derigging

NO ONE WINS EVERY RACE THEY ENTER, AND SOME RACES ARE OVER almost as soon as they begin. A problem with equipment, a poorly executed start, and with hours and even days of competition ahead of them, a crew must fight the deflating sense that the race is already over. As in life, sailors tend to make their own luck; they stay focused and wait for the breaks that shine on those who do not dismiss their possibility. Even when the day has been lost, they stick with it. There is little more impressive in sailing than the crew that straggles across the finish line, hopelessly behind the leaders, completing the task it had taken on rather than turning back for a warm port when the cause was plainly hopeless.

When you make it your calling to pursue this kind of people, you have to be as patient and as stoical as they are. I have spent many days on the water, baking under relentless sun or enduring poor conditions, and had nothing to show for it. I have attended days-long events without producing a single image that I would consider qualified for publication. It is easy to simply document an event, regardless of the conditions, but it is another thing altogether to capture the elusive shot, the one photograph that has something unique to say. I search for that shot every day I am on the water. I am still searching for the perfect image.

Plate Notes

All the images in this book were shot with Canon 35mm cameras and lenses. Various systems have been used over the years; most currently, the Canon EOS system, with four primary lenses: 28–80mm f2.8–f4L, 70–200mm f2.8L, 300mm f2.8L, and 500mm f4.5L. For images shot up to and including 1991, the film used was Kodachrome 64; after 1991 it was Fuji Velvia.

The following are detailed descriptions of the photographs, listed by page number.

14 Aerial of Farr-designed Mumm 36s at the leeward mark. 1995 Southern Ocean Racing Conference (SORC), Miami.

16 Maxi yachts *Vanitas*, *Longobarda*, and *Matador* rounding a gybe mark during the 1990 Maxi Yacht Series, Miami.

17 *Bladerunner* (Reichel/Pugh 48) takes a sharp turn during the 1988 Kenwood Cup, Hawaii.

18–19 50-footer *Insatiable* (Nelson/Marek 49) makes the turn, 1994 Key West Race Week, Key West, Florida.

20 Corel 45 *Atalanti* rounds the windward mark. 1997 SORC, Miami.

21 Mixed fleet rounding the windward mark. 1997 SORC, Miami.

22–23 Maxi yacht *Kialoa* (Frers 80) during a takedown. 1988 Maxi Worlds, Newport, Rhode Island.

24 Mumm 36 *Jameson 3* has a bit of trouble with the spinnaker at the leeward mark. 1996 Key West Race Week.

25 International Level Class (ILC) 40 *Growler* (Allan Andrews design) at the leeward mark. 1994 Kenwood Cup, Hawaii.

26 Corel 45 (Farr design) *Faster K-Yote* during the 1997 SORC, Miami.

27 Maxi yachts *Sorcery*, *Il Moro*, *Ondine*, and *Matador* round the gybe mark. 1988 Kenwood Cup, Hawaii.

28–29 Maxi yacht *Windward Passage* (Frers 82, Australia) rounds the leeward mark. 1988 Kenwood Cup, Hawaii.

30 Mumm 36 *Corum* rounds the leeward mark. 1994 Kenwood Cup, Hawaii.

31 ILC Maxi yacht *Falcon 2000* (Nelson/Marek 78, USA). 1996 Kenwood Cup, Hawaii.

32–33 *Rubin* (Germany) rounds the leeward mark during the 1993 Champagne Mumm Admiral's Cup, Cowes, UK.

34 International America's Cup Class (IACC) yacht *Young America* prepares to set during the third round robin of the 1995 Citizen Cup, San Diego.

35 Takedown on *Predator* during leeward mark rounding. 1993 Key West Race Week.

36–37 Fleet rounding the mark. 1993 Admiral's Cup, Cowes, UK.

38–39 Fleet of International 12-Metres competing in the 1986 12-Metre World Championship, Fremantle, Australia.

40–41 *Perestroika* dwarfed by the mark during the 1992 Kenwood Cup, Hawaii.

42 *Idler*, *Numbers*, and *Drumbeat* make the approach and turn at the windward mark. 1995 SORC, Miami.

43 International Offshore Rule (IOR) 50-footer *Heaven Can Wait* (Farr 50, Australia) during the 1990 Kenwood Cup, Hawaii.

44–45 Dennis Conner steering *Stars & Stripes* during the 1987 America's Cup, Fremantle, Australia.

46 Mumm 36 *Zamboni* during a takedown at the leeward mark. 1994 Kenwood Cup, Hawaii.

47 IOR 50-footers during the 1992 50-Foot World Championship, Sardinia, Italy.

48 Carl Lessard onboard the J-Class yacht *Endeavour* during a 1989 match race with *Shamrock* in Newport, Rhode Island.

50 U.S. Soling team Brad Dellenbaugh, Steve Calder, and Dave Curtis shoot off the starting line during the 1992 Olympic Classes Regatta, Miami.

51 Silver medalists Rod Davis and Don Cowie racing their Olympic-class Star boat. 1992 Kiel Race Week, Kiel, Germany.

52 Crewmember up the rig attempting to fix a broken batten on the IACC yacht *Ville de Paris* (France) during the 1992 Louis Vuitton Cup, San Diego.

53 Timing the set on IACC yacht *Team New Zealand* during the 1995 America's Cup, San Diego.

54 Etchells crew Mike Law, Simon Barnes, and Charlie Pitcher jump off the starting line during the 1994 Etchells North American Championship, Newport, Rhode Island.

55 Takedown on *Lola Bombon* during the 1996 SORC, Miami.

56–57 Maxi yacht *Matador* during the 1990 Maxi Yacht Series, Miami.

58 Crewmember up the mast on the Maxi yacht *Boomerang* (Frers 80, USA) tries to free a jammed halyard during the 1996 St. Francis Big Boat Series, San Francisco.

59 Onboard a multi-hull Tornado with Henry Bossett and Mike O'Brien during the Tornado World Championship in Kingston, Ontario, Canada.

60 Al Smith takes down the headsail on the IACC yacht *New Zealand* during the 1992 Louis Vuitton Cup, San Diego.

61 Maxi yacht *Matador* tacking close to the Gulf Stream during the 1990 Miami Maxi Regatta.

62–63 Australian 18-Foot Skiff *Ella Bache* competing in the 1996 Australian 18-Foot World Championship, Auckland, New Zealand.

64–65 Maxi yacht *Exile* (Reichel/Pugh 66, Hong Kong) on her way upwind. 1996 Kenwood Cup, Hawaii.

66 Spinnaker change onboard the IACC yacht *Nippon* (Japan). 1994 IACC World Championship, San Diego.

67 Two crewmembers conversing during a long day of two-boat testing on the IACC yacht *oneAustralia* in Southport, Australia, 1994.

68 Soling fleet reaching for the finish line. 1996 Olympic Classes Regatta, Miami.

69 Dennis Conner steering the 12-Metre *Stars & Stripes* (USA) during the 1987 America's Cup, Fremantle, Australia.

70 Maxi yacht *Longobarda* with bowman out on the pole sets up for a chute change during the 1990 Maxi Yacht Series, Miami.

71 Canadian two-tonner yacht *Evergreen* (C&C design, Canada) charges off the starting line during the 1979 Admiral's Cup, Cowes, UK.

72–73 Australian 18-Foot Skiff racing during the 1987 World Championship on the Swan River in Western Australia.

74–75 Bowman onboard *Jubilation* (Frers 54, USA) during the 1984 Big Boat Series, San Francisco.

76 Bowman on the IACC yacht *Il Moro* (Italy) calling the starting line. 1991 IACC World Championship, San Diego.

77 *Falcon* (Tripp 50, USA) in big offshore breeze. 1994 SORC, Miami.

78 *Longobarda* (Farr 80, Italy) jumps off a wave at the windward mark during the 1990 Maxi Regatta, Newport, Rhode Island.

80–81 *Love a' Luck* (Elliott 39, Japan) springs through a wave on approach to the windward mark. 1994 Kenwood Cup, Hawaii.

82 12-Metre *America II* flying on a wave during the 1986/87 Louis Vuitton Cup, Fremantle, Australia.

83 Maxi yachts *Sorcery* (Gary Mull 82, USA) and *Boomerang* (Frers 81, USA) power reaching on San Francisco Bay. 1984 St. Francis Big Boat Series.

84 *Georgia* (Farr 43, New Zealand) surfing on a wave during the 1996 Kenwood Cup, Hawaii.

85 Ken Read and crew surfing. 1994 Etchells North American Championship, Newport, Rhode Island.

86–87 Al Smith on the bow of *oneAustralia* prepares the spinnaker pole just as the genoa halyard breaks on approach to the windward mark during the 1994 IACC, San Diego.

88 IOR 50-footer *Will* (Farr 50, Japan) on a downwind ride during the 1990 50-Foot World Championship, Newport, Rhode Island.

89 *Eighty-Seven* (Farr 47, Australia) surfing during the 1994 Kenwood Cup, Hawaii.

90 Melges 24s catch a breeze in San Francisco during the 1994 Melges 24 North American Championship.

91 Ed Baird on an International 14 takes a nose-dive during the 1990 Ultimate Yacht Race, San Francisco.

92–93 *Longobarda* snaps a rig during the 1990 Maxi Regatta, Newport, Rhode Island.

94 Melges 30 rocketing downwind during the 1995 SORC, Miami.

95 Mumm 36 *Thomas I Punkt* (Germany). 1994 SORC, Miami.

96 Melges 24s reaching towards San Francisco during the 1994 Melges 24 North Americans.

97 Neck and neck at the windward mark, 1994 Kenwood Cup, Hawaii.

98 Maxi yacht *Boomerang* churns up the bay during the 1984 St. Francis Big Boat Series, San Francisco.

99 Jeff Kent speeds by on a DN Iceboat in Plymouth, MA, 1989.

100 Maxi yacht *Il Moro* power reaching during the 1988 St. Francis Big Boat Series, San Francisco.

101 12-Metres *Victory*, *Courageous*, *True North*, *Australia II*, and *Azzura* tackle big breeze and seas during the 1986 12-Metre World Championship, Fremantle, Australia.

102–103 Two-tonner *Winsome Gold* goes on a roller coaster ride on the Solent during the 1979 Admiral's Cup, Cowes, UK.

104 Mumm 36s split tacks downwind in big swells. 1994 Key West Race Week.

106 Maxi yachts *Kialoa* (Ron Holland 81, USA), *Boomerang* (Frers 81, USA), and *Ragamuffin* (Frers 76, Australia). 1984 Pan Am Clipper Cup, Hawaii.

107 Headsail change on *Falcon* during the 1994 St. Francis Big Boat Series, San Francisco.

108 12-Metres *Victory*, *Courageous*, and *True North* competing in the 1986 12-Metre World Championship, Fremantle, Australia.

109 J-Class yacht *Shamrock* glides along with an all-star crew during a 1989 match race with *Endeavour*, Newport, Rhode Island.

110 IACC yacht *oneAustralia* just on the edge of a storm while training in Southport, Australia, 1994.

111 ILC Maxi yacht *Sayonara* (Farr 79) on approach to the leeward mark during the 1996 Kenwood Cup, Hawaii.

112 Fleet of Mumm 36s glides downwind in turquoise seas off Miami during the 1995 SORC.

113 Fleet of Mumm 36s parades downwind, 1995 SORC, Miami.

114 IACC yacht *Espana* during the 1992 Louis Vuitton Cup, San Diego.

115 Mumm 36 setting off for a long night during the Molokai Race of the 1994 Kenwood Cup, Hawaii.

116–117 Fleet of 50-footers sailing downwind in a turquoise sea during the 1990 50-Foot Regatta, Miami.

118 IACC yacht *oneAustralia* training in Southport, Australia, for the 1995 America's Cup.

119 *Full Cry*, *Falcon*, and *Infinity* charging upwind in big offshore breeze, 1994 SORC, Miami.

120 Maxi yachts lap the small boats during the 1986 Kenwood Cup, Hawaii.

121 Fleet of Etchells sailing in big swells during the 1994 Etchells North American Championship, Newport, Rhode Island.

122 Two-tonner *Shockwave* (New Zealand) just after rounding the windward mark. 1994 Kenwood Cup, Hawaii.

123 Fleet of Star boats leaps off the starting line during the 1992 Olympic Classes Regatta, Miami.

124 Ultra Light Displacement Boat (ULDB) *Taxi Dancer* (Reichel/Pugh 70) close tacking among competitors on San Francisco Bay. 1989 St. Francis Big Boat Series.

126–127 One Design 48s (Reichel/Pugh 48) on one course while the Maxi yachts cut through on a different course. 1996 St. Francis Big Boat Series, San Francisco.

128 Fleet of Maxi yachts reaching towards Nassau, Bahamas, during the 1982 SORC.

129 Heading for Alcatraz, ULDB *Chance* (Santa Cruz 70) ducks under *Pyewacket* (Nelson/Marek 68). 1990 St. Francis Big Boat Series.

130 IACC yachts *oneAustralia* and *Nippon* competing in the 1994 IACC World Championship, San Diego.

131 Fleet of DN Iceboats on the starting line during the 1989 DN World Championship somewhere on Lake Champlain in Vermont.

132–133 IOR 50-footers heading upwind during the 1992 50-Foot World Championship, Sardinia, Italy.

134 *Springbok* (Farr 50, USA) approaches Diamond Head during the 1988 Kenwood Cup, Hawaii.

135 *Infinity* (Nelson/Marek 49, USA) tacks out from shore during the Kaula Race of the 1996 Kenwood Cup, Hawaii.

136–137 Fleet of IOR 50-footers lines up for the start of the 1991 Lymington Cup, Lymington, UK.

138 Congestion at the windward mark as a fleet of 50-footers prepares to set spinnakers. 1990 50-Foot World Championship, Newport, Rhode Island.

139 Fleet of IOR 50-footers reaching during the 1989 Key West Race Week.

140 Picking the best spot on the line, the fleet lines up during the 1989 Key West Race Week.

141 *Impetuous*, *Magistri*, and *Rubin* reaching out of the Solent during the 1979 Admiral's Cup, Cowes, UK.

142–143 *Stars & Stripes* tuning up in Fremantle, Australia, just prior to the 1987 America's Cup.

144 DN Iceboats at rest at the end of the day during the 1989 DN World Championship, Lake Champlain, Vermont.

145 *Camouflage* (Frers 44, USA) gives way to commercial shipping traffic during the St. Francis Big Boat Series, San Francisco.

146 Spinnaker parade down San Francisco Bay during the 1988 St. Francis Big Boat Series.

148 Fleet of J-80s reaching during the round-the-island race. 1993 Block Island Race Week, Rhode Island.

149 Bowman leading a new spinnaker out the end of the pole on the Maxi yacht *Boomerang* during the 1996 St. Francis Big Boat Series, San Francisco.

150–151 *Geronimo* leads the fleet downwind during a classic San Francisco day with a cool breeze, sun, and fog. 1984 St. Francis Big Boat Series.

152 Overhead view of *Falcon* steaming downwind during the 1994 SORC, Miami.

153 Big seas appear to swallow the One Design 48 class during the 1997 SORC, Miami.

154 *Lobo* (Reichel/Pugh 42) leads the fleet during the 1985 St. Francis Big Boat Series, San Francisco.

155 *Bright Star* (Nelson/Marek 46) hoisting the chute during the 1996 Key West Race Week.

156 12-Metres *French Kiss* and *America II* during the 1986/87 Louis Vuitton Cup, Fremantle, Australia.

157 Eight storeys up a 106-foot mast, a crewmember aboard the IACC yacht *France* 5 searches for wind lines and shifts on the 1995 America's Cup course, San Diego.

158 IOR 50-footer *Promotion* (Frers 50) under full steam during the 1993 Admiral's Cup, Cowes, UK.

159 ILC Maxi yacht *Falcon 2000* (Nelson/Marek 78) having a close encounter with Maxi yacht *Boomerang* (Frers 80). 1996 Kenwood Cup, Hawaii.

160 One Design 48s strut down San Francisco Bay during the 1996 St. Francis Big Boat Series.

161 Maxi yacht *Falcon 2000* (Nelson/Marek 78, USA) on a downwind ride during the 1996 Kenwood Cup, Hawaii.

162 Perfect symmetry as the fleet reaches towards the Bay Bridge during the 1985 St. Francis Big Boat Series, San Francisco.

163 IACC yacht *America*[3] during the 1994 IACC World Championship, San Diego.

164 Power reaching on San Francisco Bay. 1984 St. Francis Big Boat Series.

165 *Numbers* (Taylor 47) catches a wave during the 1997 SORC, Miami.

166 Sunset shot of a crewmember up the rig of the 12-Metre *Kookaburra*. 1987 America's Cup, Fremantle, Australia.